Anthony **David** Crawford

David was born in Haverton Hill, County Durham. His father worked in the local shipyard & his mother looked after the house & her father, David grandfather a retired salt worker originally from Winsford in Cheshire. David was educated at the local state school before qualifying to attend the Technical College in Stockton on Tees. From here he started work at Dorman Long Steel Company as an Apprentice Engineering Draughtsman. Over the years he has worked for a number of companies, building Blast Furnaces & Nuclear Power stations before becoming a freelance designer in the oil & gas industry. He & his wife Margaret were married in 1973 & live in Marton in Cleveland, having tried a number of sports over the years, David finally found ten pin bowling. He eventually reached a standard where he was selected to represented Durham County in National tournaments.

Poems are a reflection of life, like a kaleidoscope always changing in colour, emotions & form. Therefore, my poetry appears in this book randomly without classification by subject, Enjoy.

A Pleasure Remembered

I sit here on a hillside with a vision spread below
Fields Trees & villages with houses set in a row
A soft breeze strokes my face as the sun warms my back
Those restful peaceful feelings, nothing do I lack
A farmer cutting hay, gathered for a winter so near
I see his tractor moving though its sound I cannot hear
But the smell of the cut grass, is already reaching me
Carried on the wind with an aroma I cannot see
I hear the calls of animals & the birds as they sing
The sound from a church tower as its bells begins to ring
Rolling peel's herald joy for a wedding couple's day
Inside the church I think about the vows they will say
I wonder about this apparition the world about me why
What is there above me beyond that big blue sky
Throughout me is tranquillity that restful state of mind
A feeling of contentment we all search to find

Ancestors

We search the past, looking for roots
Seeking the paths, trod by ancestor's boots
Their lives were not easy, times they were hard
But the history they made, is now just marked on a card
Each Generation, progresses, improves
Ever striving for more, upward they move
The tin bath on the wall, is now a room off the hall
And the garden loo, is now en-suite too
But as things get better, do they improve
We gain more possessions, but what do we lose
The world all about us, who's beauty we've shun
By wasting our time, with things we think won
We chase after Mammon, believing it's real
Our friends and their company, things we feel
This is worth more, than money can buy
So don't let it go, don't say, its goodbye

Artist Engineer

I am an Artist who cannot paint
I don't need a canvas on which to create
My art takes form in alloy, wood & steel
Beautiful shapes that are ever so real
There's the Cutty Sark & its graceful lines
Brunel Clifton Bridge, speak of a different time
The wonderful Forth Bridge with its stark frame
A Nations favourite of World-Wide fame
Wrens mighty St Paul's built 300 years ago
A thing of beauty everyone knows
The Golden Gate Bridge, the Eifel Tower
My list goes on, do you have an hour
All of my Hero's who built near & far
Artists just different from Auguste Renoir

Autumn

The summer Suns warmth is fading.
Leaves are turning brown & red
Windblown into a corner
Hedgehogs gather them up for a bed
In crevices gather the lacewings
To overwinter out of the storms
With ladybirds huddled beside them
In niches they'll all be warm
Now the birds & squirrels need feeding
To survive they need water, nuts & seeds
Help them live through the winter
Give them their daily feed
No longer is there dew upon the grass
Instead, there is glistening ice
Looking ever so pretty
As from autumn to winter we pass

A Book

There something you'll find nowhere else but a book
A tale of adventure, a murder, a thieving crook
You don't need a picture or a moving film reel
They're all in your mind & they're ever so real
And those that read it never see it the same
Every picture's different it's all in your brain
Will a Kindle replace it I'm not sure about that?
I've never known a books battery go flat

Books

I've collected these friends over many years
And all have been good for my head
They fill me with fears they fill me with tears
And all have shared my bed
But don't get upset there's nothing amiss
I read all my books like this
There are stories of people & the lives they led
Adventuress tales that will fill you with dread
Fairies & creatures from a far-off land
Stories of hero's & deeds very grand
Just open a book & read the first page
You'll be totally caught in its literary cage

Brief Close Encounter

A long time ago, to Denver I flew
To program Computers, a job very new
For weeks we were there, in air so rare
And at a view of the Rockies, we'd sit & we'd stare
Weekends we'd go to where, glaciers once flow
To take in the vistas, & to gasp at the show
There was Boulder, Lake Granby then up to the peak
Hungry for more of this beauty, to seek.
Here on the rim, where we could see best
Was a sight to put, our expectations to the test
The valley below, was in full autumnal glow
And a silence so loud, on us began to grow
Then from the corner of my wandering eye
A shape that was not natural, I did espy
It was circular, shiny & in the sunlight so bright
Just above the trees, but it didn't seem right
It just seems float there, it didn't try to hide
Then we noticed the windows, all down one side
We drove down that hillside, we had to see more
It seemed to grow bigger, leaving us in awe
Could this be science fiction, has ET come for me
Then as we reached where it was in the trees
There it stood on four legs, with one central pillar
No brief close encounter, just some one's forest villa

Buildings

A building says a lot, about our Town
It tells of quality, that's no longer found
It speaks of a time, in our glorious past
When people-built things, meant to last
They had style & beauty, proportion & form
When grace & elegance were the norm
Grand Georgian windows, with carvings above
That shows they were built, with skill & love
Out towns civic pride, for the whole world to see
It shouts "This is us", just come look at me
If you want to see beauty stop looking at your feet
Raise your head up see the grandeur of the street
The sight you'll behold, will really astound
And it'll be here long after, you're not around

The Tees

The Tees is my River
It tells people, where I'm from
I've seen it over, eighty years
You'll be amazed, how quick it's gone
Once there was industry, on both of its banks
Making things for the whole wide World
For which the workers gave, much thanks
We lived on a main road, where the trucks ran to and fro
Then the railway just behind it, that was always on the go
Beyond that at the Shipyard, there was riveting all day long
And the ICI there beside it, singing its own strange song
But despite this industrial music, I slept soundly my bed
Though as a drifted off to sleep, there was noise in my head
The sound of workers blasting, in the Anhydrite mine
A thousand feet below my bed
Our world was filled with smoke and smells
Which at the time, was not thought obscene
The river ran with toxic waste, Red and Blue and Green
The Cleveland Hills are visible, on good days with no smog
But on bad days you could not see, the end of the lead
Where there should have been our Dog
But now were Eco Friendly our sky's as clear as Gin
Though when I remember how it was
I still break out in a grin

Children

Children, a new generation the future unwritten
Hopes & ambition, but all in transition
Innocents, accepting all that they find
Loving the world, letting it flood their minds
Danger's unseen, hard lessons to be learned
Relatives supporting their stumbles & falls
Encouraging aspirations, not building walls
New emerging adults, warts & all

Children

Children, the future, what we used to be
Looking for guidance from you & me
A slate & chalk with nothing written there
Heads full of spaces to store memories they'll share
Eye's wide in wonder at things they view
Then mouths full of questions what, where, who
The beauty the innocence so fragile so rare
Like a tender young plant for which we must care
Teach them to love & right from wrong
Then their lives will be complete & hopefully long

Christmas Fairy

I am the Christmas Fairy & I sit atop the tree
How the children love to see me, squeals of glee
But this year will be different, I am very sad to say
I can't be found to take my place it's going to spoil the day
I've fallen from my box in the dark below the stair
Behind the dusty water pipes & no one knows I'm there
The tree is dressed & so complete, but missing me on top
They've searched & searched for me all day
But at midnight they must stop
In the shadows I see six shining eye's
In the darkness hiding me
The mice have come to help, to get me to the tree
They lift me from my hiding place & dust me down
We'll place in your rightful place & polish up your crown
They carry me across the floor & their feet go pitter pat
We must work silently boy's, try not to wake the cat
Climbing through branches they pass the fairy paw to paw
Slowly lads be quiet, is that someone at the door
Now they're at the top, their work is nearly done
The fairy sits in pride of place her crown shines like the sun
Morning comes to such a noise, the children with surprise
How did the fairy get there, comes the inquisitive cries?
The house mice know the answer, tears in their eyes

The loss of the Redcar Blast Furnace that I helped build

Cold Steel

The furnace stack is cold and the tuyere's no longer blow
The tap hole is wide open, but in the runners there's no flow
The clay gun is empty, there's nothing for it to do
Just like the workers who were, this furnaces mighty crew
It is owned by foreign nationals and when recession strikes
They close down our works, and tell us 'On your bikes'
With no money in workers pockets, we lose the tax they pay
Instead of adding to the world, they're down Job Centre way
But if we lose this giant, where will the country go
When it needs to build steel structures, does anybody know
Were no longer self-sufficient, in anything we need
So now we'll be wide open, to exploitation and greed

Cost of War

The cost of war so plain to see
Beneath the fields lie boys like me
Plain white stones carved with pride
Mark the place of those who died
They rather hoped that they'd survive
But fate would prove to be too hard
They came they served & paid the fee
An awful price for you & me
So please remember what they gave
Each time you pass the soldier's grave

A View of War

I look across a field that should be green
But see a sight, that's quite obscene
Thousands of head stones, set in rows
Mark out the young men, who lay below
Each one their countries future, all cut short
Leaving families in pain, empty, fraught
Young men they nurtured saw them grow
Cut down in their prime, why need it be so
What do we gain by this senseless slaughter
If we don't know now, we really ought to

Days to Remember

Halcyon days when I was a tyke
Short trouser days of riding my bike
Not a care in the world me & my mates
Roaming the lanes, everything's great
Days by the creek, climbing trees
Plenty of bruises & scuffs on my knees
But there comes a time in every boy's life
When he has to face up to the truth
He's no longer a boy, he's become a youth
That first pair of long trousers & the Blazer too
Looking in the mirror at a vision that's new
Gone are the days when life was so free
I must face up to the life of grown up me

Dialect

I am told I speak funny that's what they say
How can I know I always talk this way
Call around my house I'll say how'ay in
At midday Its dinner, not lunch is that a sin
In winter when the weathers really nitherin
A hand knitted Ganzy stops me shivverin
To me a sparrow will always be a spuggy
Four wheels & a plank is called a bogie
Giving someone a lift on my bike is a croggy
Then on the beach I would wear my swimming cossie
Running down the street with a stick & a booler
Or a pocket full of alleys to take to school
Then when I write left handed, I'm a cuddy wifter
While me Da's down the club having a snifter
It's my accent, my dialect, call it what you may
That's the way I talk It's the way it'll stay

Elsham Wolds Bomber Boys

They came with the dawn, in innocence drawn
To fight off the Hun, until victory was won
But winnings not soon, as they will find
Only death and destruction, to pray on the mind
Their posting is One Group, in Bomber Command
A newly built airfield, fresh hewn from the land
High on the hill, it's Elsham Wolds Drome
This bleak remote Base, is to be their new home
How long they will live here's, in the lap of the gods
Their whole reason for living, is beating the odds
Just ordinary young men, performing extraordinary deeds
To face down Jerry, a whole world to be freed
They're Just a sprog crew, with a great deal to learn
The respect of their fellows, they will have to earn
There's thirty long trips, to drop bombs by the ton
Then they'll get a respite, their tour will be done
They first flew the Wimpy, in 41-42
Then came the Halifax, which needed more crew
Only five months later, came the Queen of the sky
The beautiful Lancaster, a real joy to fly
Were a family of seven, and we fly close to heaven
But our life can be hell, as we brave shot and shell
Night fighters, flak, and the dreaded searchlight

They're all out to get us, and cancel our night
Aircrews at the sharp end are facing the flak
But the ground crews are waiting, till they come back
Then they'll service their kites, making sure they're fit
To go back tomorrow, they're doing their bit
Were back in our billets, and it's cold in my bed
Though the pot belly stove, is glowing bright red
Fun in the billets, there's a little horseplay
But we'll all be quiet, for young Bob to pray
Young Bob Thomas, was Browning's rear gunner
Only nineteen years old, the girls thought a stunner
But the last Raid to Berlin, he met his end
Fighting off a 109, defending his friends
The airfield abounds, with people filling a need
Cooks in the kitchen, preparing our feed
There's Packers of chutes, we hope we won't use
And the MT drivers, who will ferry our crews
Doc Henderson's our medic, his first name is Bob
At curing our ache's he's the best in the job
He looks for the Twitch, a sure sign of strain
Then he'll give you a rest, before you fly again
Our free time is spent, in Scunny's Oswald bar
The 'Barnetby Flyer', will get us that far
But if we should miss it, we'll not get our flagon
The Doc he will take us, in the stations Blood Wagon
We have a night off and the urge for a Jig
So, get out the bikes, were all off to Brig
We'll down a few jars, in the Gladiator or Bull

Then it's into the dance we're all on the pull
The Base had its characters, now you will see
There was Cy Grant the lawyer, and talent had he
He would sing News calypso's, on national TV
Then there's Don Charlwood, a writer so bright
He went back to Oz, to pen 'No Moon Tonight'
The 'Mad Belgian' Van Rolleghem, 70 missions he flew
He would be an Air Marshall, in his own air force too
There was Winco Ken Wallis, of Autogyro fame
He gave James Bond, that Little Nell plane
There's old Jack and young Jack, Spark and Mackay
One on the ground, the other up in the sky
There were others, not famous, they just did their bit
On Cenotaph stones, you can find their names writ
She was Tall and Elegant, she stole young men's hearts
A Bomber legend, more than the sum of her parts
M Mother flew 140 trips, they're all marked on her card
But still she ended her days, in a breakers scrap yard
She was a Lancaster Bomber that flew like a dream
So, thank you Roy Chadwick and the Avro design team

Flower

I am standing here in this foreign land
Among Daisies & Dandelions ever so bland
I arrived as a seed in a migrating bird's rear
Deposited on the ground a dropping right here
With my own supply of Guano I soon start grow
With long slender stems two, three or four
My flowers are beautiful and very unique
I 'm ever so rare, with diligence you must seek
My petals of lilac stretch out like wings
With the body of a Bee but without its sting
I'm a beautiful Bee Orchid but if you see me
Remember I'm protected so don't pick me

Flowers

Flower, Flower standing there in the wood
No one to see you even though they should
Only the Bee's who collect your pollen
Appreciate your beauty, they visit often
But one secret admirer who knows your worth
An elderly woodsman now large of girth
He recalls your first meeting when he was young
And returns each year your beauty he can't shun

Freedom

Freedom, what does it mean to you
An animal in the wild not kept in a Zoo
To live without fear at peace with the world
Enjoying your life just letting it unfurl
Your thoughts & speech flowing free
Not having to think, who is watching me
Treasure these freedoms, guard them with care
There are those who would steal them, so beware

Hero's

What is a Hero who can tell
One man's reaction to a vision of hell
An instant response to save a friend in peril
Disregard for his own life to thwart the Devil
But in life there are Hero's all around
Just look to see, they are easily found
Looking after the sick & elderly too
They just get on with it, what a crew
In nearby care homes or a hospital ward
With compassion & care for little reward
They remember these old & sickly folk
Were once young like them & not a joke

Friendly Cat

I am your Cat I am not your pet
I am your friend, remember that
I don't take orders or go on a lead
I don't do tricks or beg for my feed
I will sit on your knee & gently purr
While you sit there & stroke my fur
I keep you calm, removing your stress
From me your pal you won't get less
My funny ways will make you guffaw
Creating memories for you to store
Because tomorrows not promised
Make the most of today

A WW2 Bomber Base ground crew's story

Ground Crew

Dawn is breaking & the ground crew are there
Waiting in the cold because they care
Aircraft are returning how many will be gone
They'll watch for them all no matter how long
They service their kites but care for the crews
But it breaks their hearts when they get bad news
An empty dispersal means a missing crew
Seven young men that they all knew
Let us hope they're all prisoners of war
Or will families get that telegram through the door
A new aircraft today & a crew of fresh-faced sprogs
Full of enthusiasm but with their empty logs
We will give them our best while they are here
But remember those lost we still hold dear

Heavens Above

As I look at our world, I can see we're a speck
On the edge of our galaxy, a microscopic fleck
We're like one grain of sand on a ten-mile beach
And to try an comprehend it, is beyond our reach
We think ourselves great, as we've flown to the moon
But in terms of the universe, it's just one step into a room
Our nearest star Centauri, is four light years away
So, leave it till tomorrow, it's too late to start today
Super Nova's, Black Holes, Quarks that go zing
On a radio telescope, you hear the universe sing
With a zillion galaxies out there, where do we start
There's light years between them, they're that far apart
Our spacecraft we need, a new way to propel
Until then we're going nowhere, or not very well
We need warp factor nine, or something of the like
Without it we may as well try, to go there on a bike
But out there I believe, is intelligent life
And my reasons are so clear
If you were that intelligent life
Would you want to visit here

High Flying

I'm sitting here relaxed, in my comfy seat
I've just had my lunch & a big gooey sweet
I'll now wash it down, with a nice red wine
I'm feeling so good, isn't life just fine
That's nothing remarkable you may say
You have your lunch, every day
But I have to say, I must disagree
Just let me explain, & you will see
We are at 30 thousand feet, with the ocean below
I have 600 companions, sat in row after row
There're spread over two decks, I can't believe what I see
As I watch a video or, even go for a pee
I stretch to look backward & see condensate trails
Like a speedboat's wash our progress it hails
Now I wonder if the Wright brothers on Kitty Hawk Sands
Thought this could be so, in their visions so grand

Holiday

A Holiday, honestly is that what you need
Or do you just want to ditch, life's stresses & greed
Languish is a quiet wood, within a leafy glade
Embrace its peace let the silence flood your mind
Delight in the tiny sounds your hearing will find
Allow natures beauty to enrich your life, be brave
You will find it's so much better than the holiday you crave

Holidays

I can't go on a holiday & just sit in the sun
It's a waste of my life & not much fun
I've got to keep busy seeing lots of sites
Experience new culture, food & bright lights
Meet local people who go out of their way
To point out the best places to eat or stay
Speak their lingo please don't be slow
They'll thank you for trying just have a go
Then at the end, of your adventure young man
You'll have more to remember than a fading tan

The Last Goodbye

The end of the summer, disappears under the plough
We watch it go, in the here and now.
A view of the tree's vivid, autumnal glow
Or the sight of the settling winter snow
Maybe the swallows, as they homeward fly
Each in its own way, a memorable goodbye
Nothings forever, no matter how you try
As we all wait for our own, last goodbye.
But it needn't be so sad, if while you are here
You leave memories for those that you hold so dear

Life's Puzzle

Life can be very traumatic
And cruel, without reason or rhyme
People we knew, have been taken
Long long before their time
Some were just at school still
Others had just started life's page
No old age pension for them
No chance to relax in old age
Like a poem with only a title
The rest just a blank page
Then when I think of my own life
And so far it's been quite long
I give thanks for the years I've had
But remember those that are gone

Love illusions

My Love of the movies, with its visions grand
Lifting plain folks from a reality very bland
It gave us a world, so much better than ours
If only a dream, that would last a few hours
There were Indians & Settlers, losing the war
Till along came the Cavalry, to even the score
Roy Rogers, Trigger & wife Dale Evans who
Showed us the West, so clean it weren't true
Then along came John Wayne, much more gritty
He brought us a reality that was not so pretty
But when Clint Eastwood in Rawhide, hit our screen
We saw Rowdy Yates, dirty, rough & mean
These were the stars, of our silver screen
And for only a Bob, we could sit & dream
Our life's so simple, with those stars above
All of them Hero's, we came to Love

Passion or Love

Passion & love are different my friends
Passion is of the moment, but love never ends
In our youth there's, attraction & passion galore
But with time you will find, love counts for much more
The years you will spend making memories of gold
Memories to recall as you both grow old
You walk down a street, holding hands all the time
Giving each other a hug, without reason or rhyme
Saying I love you, with no prompting at all
Even though you can drive, each other up the wall
But Love is what holds you together for life
In the end Its what makes you man and wife

Chowhound & Manna from Heaven

Its April 45 we have the Jerries on the run
But for the people of Holland, life's far from fun
The retreating Hun's, taken all their food & cattle
So, life has become, a survival battle
Starvation is staring them, all in the face
Who will help them stay, in the human race
There's only Tulip bulbs left, to grind into flour
To make bread with a taste that's very sour
When the allies find out, they hatch a plan
To feed the Dutch, every woman child & man
They warn old Jerry, we are coming with food
Don't get in our way, interference you'll rue
We fill up our bombers with food in sacks
There's flour for bread & meat to make snacks
At 90 knots & 200 ft, look for people near an empty patch
Then open the bomb doors & the food is dispatched
The RAF & Eighth air force flew, many trips that were long
To feed the people in the fields where they all throng
Laying sheets on the ground, the Dutch show their joy
Spelling out simple words like, 'Thank you Boy's'
These battle-hardened crews, with tears in their eyes
Returned to their Bases, chests swelled with Pride
Now seventy years on, the Dutch still recall
The days when food, from the skies began to fall
They still care for our boys, who never came home

Remember their sacrifice, as if they were their own

Missionaries

Missionary, Missionary around the World you plod
Looking for people to convert to your God
But why should they listen, they have Gods of their own
So go back home & leave them alone
But should you continue to pester this lot
Don't be surprised if you end up in a pot.
The American Indians have the spirit of Mother Earth
They enjoy its beauty, appreciate its worth
They don't build factories or chase after mans greed
They only take from it, what they need
The Asian Indians have Vishnu & Shiva
Who's to say they were wrong, they're still believers
Thai's Buddha believes in reincarnation, I'd feel a chump
If I believed in this & came back as Donald Trump
Now I have only one thing to say, to end this list
I thank God, I'm an Atheist

Moments to Remember

Our life is rolling along just fine
Then something awful happens in time.
I remember the day that Kennedy Died
The fearful knots that gripped my insides
Joyful memories of a fairy tale wedding
That ends in a tunnel with no happy ending
The night I watched as we land on the Moon
But we won't explore the universe very soon
Medical breakthroughs good news for some
Too late for others whose time has come
Our world will go on despite news good or bad
Believe me I've seen it since I was a lad

My Home

I remember my home when I was a lad
Me my Grandpa my Mum & Dad
These were the days just after the war
Memories of the bombing tender & raw
Food was so short we grew our own
Down on the allotment not far from home
Dad was still working building ships
While Mum was cooking up something with chips
Sundays were the best days & Mums baking skills
Meat pies, curd tarts, fairy cakes fit the bill
These feed us all day & in the weeks Bait Box go
No wonder around the middle I grow
Grandad from Winsford would tell me tales of his youth
But I'm not quite sure they were all the truth
Sitting on his knee I remember those, comforting smells
Pipe Baccy, Mints & Fiery Jack, rubbed in well
Weekends Dad & I, in dawns early gloom
Would search the fields, for the tasty mushrooms
In summer we gathered the brambles from the bush
To supplement our food, life was quite tough
There was no TV to watch or Nintendo to play
Only the Radios, Home Service or the Light Wave
There was Henry Halls music & Billy Cottons Band
Not much now but then, the best in the Land
It's all gone now, apart from here in my head

Though there are things that can trigger, the life I once led

My Life

What's is life about, I haven't a clue
I didn't get instructions, did you?
My life like footprints in a fresh fall of snow
I just make them up as on my way I go
Around me are people, who seem to know the way
Or are they like me, but just afraid to say
I've made many mistakes, as my life evolves
But each is a problem, I have had to resolve
So, I try to learn, from these errors in my life
Then start again, to make my world without strife
Eventually you will become an expert my friend
But It will take you a lifetime & it will be right to its end

My Poetry

I love to write poetry, but I'll never be a Bard
I don't use silver spoon word's, I'm more Tin bath in the yard
I love to read the Night Mail, or the Dying of the Light
But just because poets are famous, they can still write tripe
Poetry should speak to people & with their lives strike a chord
Otherwise, when folks read it, they will soon become bored
I love to write about people & the lives that they've had
Sometimes it's about happiness other times very sad.
But that's what life's all about & it won't go away
Try to make the best of it there is always a piper to pay
There are poems about school days & the universe high above
But I would like to write with more passion, of life & love
Maybe that will come with time & I'll write something grand
Till then I'll just keep writing, till the pen falls from my hand

My Wife

Now I am a married man for forty years or more
Before that I was single & believe me, it could be a chore
Yes, I went boozing with my mates & chased all the girls
But soon came to realise, this just left my head in a whirl
I needed something more, a meaning to my life
I realised what was missing, I needed a wife
Now that's the easy part, any fool can get wed
But I was looking for someone, to share more than my bed
Then one night a friend & fiancé, were having a do
Lots of people present, but not many I knew
She was not very tall but a beauty none the less
We danced & talked, then I took he home in a while
Twelve months later we were walking down the aisle
The rest is history & I wouldn't change a day
We've had our ups & down & health scares along the way
We've both stared into life's abyss
But we have weathered the storms, to enjoy wedded bliss
We have walked hand in hand all our married life
To me that's how it should be as man & wife
I love you is what I say each day & tell her how I care
One day I may not be able to do it & that makes me scared
We make every day count, like it may be our last
So there'll never be regrets about what's been our past

My Life

The world that was, I know not off
Nor know of the world that's to come
But as I am here, I see quite clear
The world that I have right now
I have no fear of what was my past
Nor have fear of what is to be
I can only enjoy, what is here & now
That's got to be enough, for me
They claim that religion is here
To make the peasants feel fine
And stop them from getting all fretful
To keep the poor buggers in line
Some say there is reincarnation
So do we just go, round and round
Just like a modern-day juke box
Always playing a different sound
I will never be able, to take control
I am just along for the ride and the view
I'd like to think there is something more
For me and you and you

A WW2 Bomber Crews tour of 30 Raids

Night Operations

The suns long gone from view
Night's gown covers the land
Ghostly silhouettes, of the Bombers crew
In fear & trepidation they stand
Their lives are on the line this night
What of tomorrow, how will the dice fall
Lady luck please be kind, treat us right
Or tomorrow shall our names be written on fates wall
Twenty-nine times we have looked death in the face
Will we complete our 30th, or stumble at the line
Many have fallen, never completing this race
Leaving empty beds without reason or rhyme
Fate has been kind; their luck has held up
A respite they've earned, relief from the fight
Others will step up to lift the winner's cup
But for them the prize they walk away with, Life

Old

Old what does it mean; let's see
Wrinkles, grey hair that is me
Aches & pains creaking bones
Difficulty hearing folks on the phone
Stronger glasses eyesight dimming
Getting slower at chasing women
Things going wrong, or dropping off
Sounds like me but please don't scoff
We used to live three score years & ten
Longer now, but it's still not if but when
So, enjoy what you have before it's gone
Let's hope we can reach that magic TON

Oliver Bertie & Blondie

It's a grey, grey morn, just before dawn
There under a tree, sits a black furry form
Two shiny bright eyes, surveys the scene
Looking for people, who won't be mean
People are moving, he's ready to run
Are they friendly, or will they shun
They are putting out food, it's a good sign
They're making soft sounds, I run & hide
They've gone inside, & I sneak back
To eat the food, a tasty snack
The next few days, they repeat this treat
Looks like a good place, to rest my feet
In no time at all, I'm sitting in splendor
They've taken me in, & they treat me tender
I sleep on a cushion & they brush my fur
They call me Oliver & I start to purr
I'm looked after by Granny & Margaret too
There's also a man who, I'm frightened will shoo
But the years pass by I've made this my home
No reason to leave, no more reason to roam
Ten years have gone by, & now Granny & I
Are moving to Thornaby, so Stockton goodbye
There's new friends to meet, like Bertie my mate
He shows me the gardens, isn't Thornaby great
For three long years we have been together
But now Bertie has gone, I miss my brother
I sit on his mat I can still smell his scent

I just wish I knew, where he went
New people have arrived, down the road
With them are two cats, or so I am told
One is Blackie, & his sister Blondie
I will wait to see, if they are friendly
Now Blondie is white, & two-tone brown
Older than I am, but quite a clown
Blackie is shy, & he never goes out
I have seen them both, as I walk about
Now Blondie & I, get along just fine
We sit on a bench, & enjoy the sunshine
Her owners are leaving, & she can't go along
So we take her in, now to us she belongs
The years slip by, & our lives are so good
But now Blondie has gone, where is my Bud
I sit all alone, & watch the people go by
They smile & wave, but they don't see me cry
Our world is changing, we are moving on
From Thornaby to Marton, let's hope its fun
My gardens big, with a copse across the road
How Bertie & Blondie, would have loved it so
Now I'm getting old, & sometimes I'm ill
They take me to the Vets, & Ann gives me a pill
This makes me feel better, so I can't complain
When you get to 19, you will see sunshine & rain.
Now Oliver's gone but we won't be sad
We remember the good time & the fun we had
Walks three times a day to see folks in the street
Chasing autumns leaves as they blow round his feet
Keeping us amused with his funny ways
Remembered forever to the end of our days

Our Family

To people a family is kids, mum & Dad
Just like my family when I was a lad
But now I'm older I am changing my view
The other folks in this world are family too
We live on this planet, the human race
All of us family just from a different place
So, let's forget colour, religion & cultures
If we continue to fight, we're just food for Vultures

This is the old part of Middlesbrough

Queens Square Buildings

I stand on Queens Square, proud as can be
I've done it since I was built, in 1903
My edifice has classic lines
That makes you stand & stare
With cornices & gargoyles
All carved, with loving care
I watch other, rise beside me
Built by shipping, coal & steel
From our Industrial revolution
Came the town's great evolution
But the war years of the Forties
Saw destruction so sad to see
By our enemies aerial sorties
But they did not damage me
The resurrection of the sixties
Built of concrete steel & glass
Put up so quickly, but with very little class
They go up, and then come down again
As changing fashion, decides their fate
They don't have my style
So, they never will be great.
I represent more than Mammon
While they're just fickle new

I'm the original, Grade Listed 2
Reflections of a day

As I lay on the beach on the warm golden sand
Its fine grains running through the fingers of my hands
I look up at the heavens & see the summer clouds scurry by
As white trails of aircraft stitch, them together in the sky
Closing my eyes. I listen to a world full of sound
Children's cries of innocence, travel across the ground
A seagull's piercing calls a mournful haunting note
Carries down the beach as on the breeze it floats
The noise of the fun fair, the rumble of the rides
Squeals from the people on the water slides
I open my eyes to take in the view as I stand
The incoming tide breaches the castles of sand
It's time to go home as the sun starts to sink
My day has gone so quick like an eyelids blink
But all is remembered like a canvas full of paint
To be recalled in the future without complaint

School Day Hero's

They say that our school days, are the best indeed?
But how could we know, we were just growing seeds
Our minds were like sponges, absorbing it all
But at times I felt, I was hitting my head on a wall
Our teacher were Veterans, from World War 2
Of far more interest, than what Columbus did too
Dates from history, which Monarch followed which
I just wanted to kick a ball, on a footy pitch
My Hero's were Chindits, Ghurkha's, people who flew
Bomber Command Airmen and the Glorious Few
Men on the Achilles, Ajax and Exeter who
Took on the Graf Spee, and Langsdorff's crew
There were the Desert Rats in Africa, giving their all
And the Burma Railway prisoners, who's treatment would appal
On the high seas there were the convoys, sailing to and fro
Facing Atlantic U Boats and the Arctic Snow
Our Veteran teachers gave us, more than learning
They taught us about the World, and left us yearning
They said we must search, around life's bends
There's a whole world of people, to make our friends
Now no longer with us, we remember them all
Harry Taylor, Mr. Gray, and Mr. Jobson who
Took us on a summer camp. to give us all a view
Of a world outside our own, that we never knew
Now we go through life evolving, as day follows night
Our lives like a Jewels facets each one shining bright
They're formed and polished by, all our friends who
Make us what we are, as we shape them too.

School Days

I remember my first day & my teacher miss Blair

The war had just finished we had no more cares

No dashes at midnight to shelter from the bombs

We could sleep sound at night & play all day long

Then the winter of 47 three long months of snow

Tramping to school early, giving our fingers a blow

Teachers spraying water, to make a slide in the yard

But when you fall on your backside that ground was hard

Sitting next to the radiators trying to warm up my toes

Trying to write down lessons but the ink won't flow

Absorbing the 3 R's because it's what makes our world tick

Learning about general knowledge so as not to look thick

Being taught respect for others & for yourself as well

Life's not going to be easy so let's get used to it now

So, when you move into the real world you'll know how

Now back in my past I remember the lessons I learned

It has served me so well as my living I have earned

My school days I remember like sunlight through clouds

With a warm happy feeling & a life of which I can be proud

Seasons of a life

The seasons of the year are reflections of my life
My childhood is the springtime, enthusiasm rife
Growing from a seed, like a sturdy tree
Where am I going, just what will I be
Then it's the summer, basking in the sun
Maturing quickly now, I'm learning how to run
Taking on responsibility, a Family & a Home
Sharing all my dreams with my wife, not alone
But as the year slips by, Autumn shows its face
I decide to take a step back, from life's rat race
Make the most of my leisure time, before winters chill
See our world around us, before someone sends the bill
Then we face our winter & winters not much fun
But to keep us warm are memories, before we are gone

Sick World

What is wrong with our World?
Why are people so sick?
It's not a medical problem
Cured by a needle's prick
They want something for nothing
But that's not the way
They must build for a future
Not just live for the day
For in time to come they will see
You lose it all, believe you me

War Memorial

Why do you stand & look at this stone
It bears my name but it is not me
I was just one of many
Who came to make a difference but
All I might have been is lost forever
Please do not let my sacrifice be a waste
Make the world I leave you a better place
If you come in remembrance of me
Bless you for your time

A North East tale of the local tribes

Smoggie

They call me a Smoggie I have to agree
For I live by the Tees as it runs to the sea.
But that's not the reason I'll try to explain
So, listen very closely I won't repeat it again
We take the smoke and the smells
Made by ICI Chemists spells
As they brew up their nylons and polymers
And were well on the way to our fame
But when we mix it with Fog
We get a foul smelly Smog
I hope I don't need to go further.
For the Geordies and Machem's
And the Chimp Chokers too
The source of our name is here.
Just look for the clue

In Memory of my great uncles who fought in the Great War.
John, James & Harry. Ashley
John sadly was killed on the first day of the
Battle of the Somme at Fricourt.

Somme Pals

Me & my Pals work hard all week
Spare time we kick a ball in the street
Not much pleasure for skint boys to seek
In this world of ours, life is so bleak
They say that the Jerries, are getting upset
Over some dead Archduke, that I've never met
But people are fighting, it's getting out of hand
So, we'll help the French, someone must make a stand
Now Lord Kitchener says, your Country needs you
My mates & I join up, were patriots too
Were named the Pals Battalion, & were off to War
But first we must train & then train some more
We are suited in Khaki & boy is it rough
When we start marching, our skin it scuffs
Our boots must be shiny, & there's Blanco to do
We all get a rifle, with a big bayonet too
Now we are trained, or so they say
We march through the town & folks shout 'Hooray'
Then it's off to the station for a train to the coast
As we say our goodbyes to those we love most
Now a trip on a ferry from, Blighty to France
Then a train to the front, through this land of romance

We all disembark near a river, called the Somme
Let's hope we won't be here very long
But this is not, our final destination
We march for miles, though a land of desolation
Here in the trenches, we are in for a shock
Keep your head down, or Jerry shoots of your block
Every where's filthy, even soldiers we meet
As we march in, they troop out, all dead beat
They are glad we are here, they need the rest
But smiling knowingly, they call 'All the best'
We huddle in our dugouts & try to sleep
But noise of the shelling our dreams defeat
We dig out holes, high in the trench wall
To keep us dry & from rats that crawl
The big push is here & Jerries so near
Only one hundred yards, each one filled with fear
Over the top, were just one step from Hell
At least if I fall, I'm with Pals I know well
Now the fighting's over, the surrender is signed
In front of the cenotaph, our troops are lined
My families here too & they all look so fine
There's a Bronze plaque with names on
Sadly, one of them is mine

Tango Sensations

We start with an embrace that has passion, grace
Then lean close together, becoming one in that space
The music breaks the silence, and we feel for the beat
Which we trace on the floor, with our souls and feet
There is no agenda, our emotions choose the moves
As Ocho's, Secadas, & Gancho's, express our mood
It all becomes hypnotic, as a trance takes command
We float round the floor to the sounds of the band
We move through shadows then into the light
As we glide round the room lost in our delight
There's sensuous gyration as she follows my lead
Not a word will be spoken there's never a need
There's movement then pauses, each plays it's part
As music & dance comes together in Art
A final crescendo and they spiral to the floor
But already inside they're craving for more

In Memory of RAF Bomber Command WW2

The Bomber Command Spire

In the glorious fields of Lincolnshire
From where our Bombers once flew
They have built a Spire, remembering the crews
In sight of the Cathedral, it will be seen for years
But the reason it's there, will bring you to tears
It's a tribute to the flowering Commonwealth seeds
Who came to defend freedom, in its hour of need
All across Europe, these seeds lay scattered
In the hope that their sacrifice, really mattered
There were fifty-five thousand, who never went home
Into the face of the Memorial, their names have been honed
So, let's stand in silence, and remember their loss
Then try to make a World, without another Cross

The Key

The key to life is simple
Just be honest & be true
Don't try to be what you're not
Just let you be you
People try to impress others
Hoping to be in the click
They only make fools of themselves
And end up looking quite sick
I don't need to be accepted
I am who I am
I'm not caviar on Biscuits
I am bread & butter with JAM
So just let those high flyer's vanish
They are as shallow as drops of rain
Look for those you share interests
You won't go very far wrong

Remembering the skies over Europe during WW2

The Cold Blue

The Cold, Cold Blue
Where young men once flew
Fighting a war for me & you
From the plains & the mountains
They answered the call
City boys & farmers one & all
To fight the war in Europe's sky
A bloody cruel battle ever so high
At 35 thousand feet its 40 below
But there's sweat on my brow is all I know
Those that were there will say it was so
It's a fearful place but still we went
Fighters attacking, Fighters to defend
Let's hope one day it will come to an end
Till then we fight on facing the flak
Please lord help bring us all back
But if we should fall remember our deeds
Bring peace to our loved ones & see to their needs
Then in the future commemorate what we did
And speak of us often when you teach our kids
Remember a soldier was once heard to say
For your tomorrow, We gave our today

Old Man

An old man stands before me
With a face that's wrinkled & worn
But in his eye's I can still see
He is far from downcast or forlorn
They show he has led a full life
He's experienced this world's pleasure & pain
He's seen all its trouble & strife
And yes! he would do it again
He's never chased after life's treasures
He's never sought out shallow fame
The simple things in his life give him pleasure
Their memories will always remain.
He always wakes up in the morning
And looks forward a whole world to see
As I look at the old man in the mirror
I can see the old man is me

Universal Wonder

Looking up at the night sky, my mind starts to race

Laying on the grass, staring out into space

The Milky Way our Galaxies swirling sweeping arc

Spinning slowly around, illuminating the dark

The startling flash of a shooting stars path

Scores the inky darkness in a terminal crash

Though what I can see, with my limited sight

The vastness of the void makes me take fright

Ursa Major, that vast region out in space

Thousands of Galaxies in a very small place

Each one like ours with Planets & Suns

Could they hold family's children, & Mums

So, as I lay here looking out at all that black

A sudden thought trouble's me

Is someone, looking back

Many years ago I wandered around a disused Bomber Base remembering how it was just after the war. Now it's paintwork weather worn & peeling the windows broken, walkways & runways with grass growing through the joints. Once bustling with people nature is reclaiming it. I was so moved I wrote the following to remember those that wrote history here.

The Old Control Tower

The wind whistles, through the Crittall frames
An Operations board covered with fading names
Echo's of footsteps on a well-worn stair
Men off into the night to who knows where
Now just a memory to the diminishing few
Who inhabited the tower when it was new
A lifetime of memories soaked into the walls
The sound of returning aircraft & radio calls
Chattering aircrew relieved to be back
Talk of fighter combats & lots of flack
Now it's a breakfast that egg & bacon treat
Then off to the billet, bed & to sleep
Tomorrow's a new day to do it all again
Yesterday's young hero's now old men

The Visit

A visit to a friend I have worked with for years
He remembers who I am, he even knows my name
We talk for hours & sometimes, there are tears
He recalls the plants we built, but I can see he has fears.
He does not know what day it is, or what he's going to do
If you ask him what he had for lunch, he hasn't got a clue
This sets him aside from the likes of me & you
The man I learned from & who taught me all I know
Is disappearing before my eyes, every time that I go
It's sad to see this strong man, become so frail & insecure
But the thing that is so frightening is there is no known cure
I have to watch him melt away & that leaves me mad
As this grand old man, reverts back to being just a lad

During WW2 the United States Army Airforce flew
from the green fields of East Anglia this poem is for them.

The Mighty Eighth

A new day dawns another mission to do
Farm boys, City Boys & Mountain men too
Putting their lives on the line without any end
A long way from home, family & friends
The Mighty Eighth with its shiny planes
All painted up, with their fancy names
Passionate Witch, the Memphis Belle
Many, many more we remember them well
Those ten-hour trips to the heart of the Reich
Rookies or old hand we all feel alike
Filled inside with that deep trepidation
Still, we press ahead with determination
Our fighter boys are circling, our lucky charm
But it's the flack we know that can do us harm
Now over the target the flack is so thick
We are on our own let's get in & out quick
Lining up for the drop, ships are taking hits
Falling out of formation shedding bits
They head for home a hope we all share
Please God let them make it is our prayer
Others are falling we look for the chutes
There's not enough, our hearts are in our boots

Families will hear of their missing folk
Some are POW's others will be heart broke
They will not be the first or the last sad to say
Fighting for a better world, a brighter new day
But the war proceeds their comrades will go on
By continuing to fight they honour those gone
They pray for the day when this war is done
Then once again become a husband or son
When they can return back home to their kin
Their own lives & a world to start again

Witch

Witch, Witch there in the wood
Are you for evil, or are you for good
Brewing your potions & chanting your rhyme
Sending people to Heaven, or to Hell for all time
Simple folk from the village, seek you for a spell
To cast off a curse, that makes them unwell
Love potions for others, or misfortune on a foe
With the Eye of a Newt, & a Frogs big Toe.
But what of your needs, there in the wood
Are you an Ogre, or just misunderstood

Troubled Soul

It's a cold winter's night & the moon is full
There's been snow all day, but now there's a lull
The guards at the main gate are waiting in fear
Will he return tonight, as he's done each year?
Then by the hanger, from the shadows he appears
The guards are wide eyed, will he come near
His uniforms old circa 42, dirty & torn he's lost one shoe
Why is he here, & if we only knew who
Walking quite slowly, he's dragging one foot
There's blood on his face, which is smeared with soot
In the snow there's no track, to mark his way
For what is he searching & why this day
Then into the shadows he fades away
Now It's the warm summer of 72
Up on the hills, there's forestry work to do
Mature trees to be cleared, fresh saplings to follow
Then well off the track, they find in a hollow
The remains of a fighter, a crumpled old wreck
From Its last war time combat, no one came to check
And there on its wing, the pilot's laid too
With his badly broken leg that's lost its shoe
He died as he fought, out there all alone
Missing in combat, was all they wrote home
On a winter sortie he went & never came back
Many young men did, though now he'll get a plaque
He was buried with honour as the military will do
Remembered by the men with which he once flew
It's a cold winter's night & the moon is full
There's been snow all day, but now there's a lull
The guards at the main gate are waiting in fear
Will he return tonight, as he's done each Year
No longer will he return, with peace he is blest
His earthly remains have been laid to rest

Who wants to live forever

I came into this life, and never knew where I'd bin
But here to look after me was all my kith and kin
They showed me an amazing world, of things to see and do
And as I absorbed it all, I grew and I grew
Then quickly I saw, there's no time to do it all
Unless I can live forever, and never hear gods call
And as I thought about it, the idea did not appeal
Although It sounds great, would it prove unreal
You would see if global warming, was the disaster they all said
Would over population see us fighting, for water and bread
You would see real space travel, and cures for all life's ills
Don't worry if it takes some time, you have eternity to fill
So, let's look at the long term, and give you all a fright
You'll be there when the world ends, however that will be
You may drop into a Black Hole, and be crushed down to a pea
Or will a Galactic crash, blow us into dust, too small to see
You'll have to spend forever, drifting round and round in space
With no one to talk to, or look you in the face
There'll be no release from this, it's forever and a day
So do you want live this never-ending hell, No Way
So, let' leave 'Who wants to live forever'
To Freddy Mercury and Queen
For to try it in the real World makes a Nightmare of a Dream

Witches

A strange, strange calling, to be a witch
We make peoples skin crawl or give them a twitch
In witch craft you'll find some are black, others white.
And most people think, we only work at night
Believe me they're wrong, were not afraid of the light
We sit round a pot, with our potions & spells
We're really washing our smalls, to get rid of the smells
We fly on a broomstick & a Black Puss we must have
He's to shows us the way, our very own CATNAV
Woman ask us for love potions, to capture a man's heart
If they'd show him some passion, he'd chase them from the start.
Being a Witch is a lonely life, no one wants a witch for their wife
We live in a hut in a dark wood & the food we eat is not so good
Eye of Newt, Toe of Frog, I'd rather have a pie & a chocolate log
We wear a black dress & a big pointy hat
It's not very bright but it matches the cat
Now Witches are a dying breed
With medical science there's no more need
So, a new job I must find, maybe
A Tea shop in the wood sounds just fine

Wonderful World

It's a wonderful world, so people say

But don't rush through it, enjoy each day

Life's simple pleasures are there all around

Lift your head up, stop staring at the ground

Smell the flowers hear the buzz of the Bees

The singing of birds, the wind in the Tree's

Life's wonderful sensations are all for free

Belonging to no one, not you or me

Lay in the dark, looking up at the sky

See a meteor trail, as it passes and dies

There are brilliant stars, hazy Nebula's too

All of them there in a sky, that's not blue

The velvet soft hiss, of the tide on the sand

As it rolls in and out, covering the land

Like the sound of the world breathing, in & out

Our wonderful world, how can there be doubt

Winter's Tale

Winter's a time to sit by the fire
Imagining in the flames our hearts desire
Nothing is real in that flickering light
Tomorrow's reality out of sight
Enjoying this time when our world is calm
Remembering things from a distant time
Sadness & Joy as our mind unwinds
Taking away those thoughts that bind
A magical moment that we try to hold
Like liquid mercury as our cares unfold
Ending with sadness in the dying coals

Fred Spencer was based at RAF Elsham Wolds in WW2.
He was ground crew of 103 Squadron. Later he would
become President of the Elsham Wolds Association

Fred's Spencer's Tribute

He stands at the memorial, as he's done for years
A poppy wreath in his hand, in the eyes are tears
He remembers young men, who gave their all
Now just a name, on a stone where they fall
They were so full of life, with youthful ambitions
But they were to suffer, the war's brutal attrition
On nights off they could be found, quaffing beer
And singing so loud, the whole town could hear
They chased the girls, who brought them much cheer
Then it's back to the bar, and quaff some more beer
But the locals forgave them, they cut them some slack
For tomorrow these lads, may not be coming back
He's on Horse Guards Parade, awaiting the call
When they're ready to start, he will March down Whitehall
It's November 11th, the Armistice day Parade
For his comrades he's come, another wreath to be laid
I recall those trips, to Mailly le Camp he made
To remember the boys, who took part in the raid
There were 255 lost, on that fearful moonlit night
They watched them all fall, from out of their sight
It's seventy long years, since they've been gone
But those who were lost, are still twentyone

I am a member of a local Poetry group In 2018 we all wrote a poem to commemorate the 100th anniversary of the Battle of the Somme. One of the members is a lady of mature years who can always be relied on to cast a different light on a subject. This I consider an excellent example of her work which I am sharing with her permission.

The Battle of the Somme

Tommy is ninety-four but his back is straight
As before the stone he stands
He traces the names of mate after mate
With brown spotted, trembling hands

Exam students with young backs bent
Over desks in a warm, close room
Answer questions on that awesome event
The air is still and quiet as a tomb

When Tommy sailed for France that day
He was aged all of nineteen
But you grow up quick so they say
When death hits your eyes right between

Remember students, date, names and facts
The General, his strategies and his deeds
Remember his famous walking attacks
Instructions a good soldier heeds

Tommy and his mates did as they were told
They walked into battle as he said
Tommy survived, managed to grow old
But most of his mates lay dead

Next question, students, how many died?
In that battle they called the Somme
One thousand, two, three, four or five?
I know we can ask old Tom

There was Scouser Joe and Geordie Jack
And Ben from down Somerset way
There was the little lad I carried on my back
He died before the end of the day

You're finished now, the end of the test
Now walk out of school don't run
If you really want to know the rest
Ask Tom, head bent in the sun

He walks between the uniform stones
With the sun beating down on his head
Then lifts his face to the sky and moans
Don't ask me, I don't know why they're dead

We didn't ask questions then you see
We just did as we were told
Don't make the same mistakes as we
Ask why, maybe you'll grow old.

Ann Peel copyright

Printed in Great Britain
by Amazon